GW00401650

STORM'S STORY

LUCY POSTGATE

Grosvenor House
Publishing Limited

This book is published by
Grosvenor House Publishing Ltd
Link House
140 The Broadway, Tolworth, Surrey, KT6 7HT.
www.grosvenorhousepublishing.co.uk

A CIP record for this book
is available from the British Library

ISBN 978-1-78623-071-3

Chapter One.

Oh Storm. Do you really want a book all of your own?

You do?

Yes.

Yes of course you do.

Storm has caused me more injury, pain, exasperation and anxiety than any other horse I have had in my care. He has been with me for seven years now and I would say he has only recently become a happy, chilled, contented chap. It took a long time to work him out.

His story goes back some time before I bought him.

Way back in 2007 the most beautiful horse in the world and my companion of 26 years died. Of course we know these things must happen, but I do not think we can ever really prepare ourselves for the event. Ottie was on her way to her 30th birthday. Somehow, I thought she would go on for ever.

Ottie was an integral part of my riding school. She was an escort horse, school mistress, excellent with children and a flamboyant 'airs above the ground horse' when required. After losing her, the riding school continued as best it could. Pupils who had pranced around the school on Ottie had to come down to earth on Bug, a New Forest pony with firm ideas of her own, or on Tippy, who had no patience with beginners. Little Lobelia (a chunky chestnut Shetland), Dylan, Miranda and Mia (all

Welsh Mountain ponies) kept the children occupied. I rode Killin (a bay, Irish Draught cross Thoroughbred mare) when we hacked out. Killin took to her role as Top Horse with pleasure. Indeed it was no more than she expected. She was a delight.

The problem was that all my clients wanted to ride her too.

It took me another two years to face the reality that I needed another proper grown-up horse. A horse I could confidently use to escort rides and use as a school mistress/master in lessons.

My horses usually find me.

This time I had to set out to look for one.

I took my daughter Alanna along to all the viewings. She would definitely have an opinion, and, being as old and creaky as I am, I needed her riding skills.

We went to see a family pet – an aged quiet grey mare, looking for a good home.

"The winters are too long," said the owner.

She was stabled when we arrived. As soon as the owner opened the stable, the mare charged out of the door, ran over the owner and made off into the cottage garden. When the mare was eventually dragged back to the stable yard (having never ever behaved like that before, of course...) she was fidgety and pushy.

"She is a lovely mare," I said, backing my way out of their yard. "I'm sure she will settle down with the right person. Just not quite what I'm looking for…"

We continued our search at a local horse dealer. They had at least three that would suit us they said. We watched the first mare being ridden (always a good idea – I am learning as I go!). The mare was uneducated, a bit nervous, but had nice paces and popped over a small jump neatly. Another good idea is to put your daughter on before yourself. Alanna rode the mare well but was told on no account was she to carry a whip. The mare was clearly very unrelaxed. Again I did not get a good feeling. The mare is only five years old and she is whip shy? We did not look at the other two.

Eventually, I bought a horse from another dealer – a friend of a friend. She had a good arrangement whereby you could return the horse and have your money back within the first week or have the horse replaced if things did not work out within three months.

I won't dwell on this unhappy episode. The horse had at least three names and two passports. He brought a virus into my yard which took six months to work its way through all the horses. That summer became known as 'the Summer of Snot'. He filled my paddocks with worms. He would go from standing to a gallop for no apparent reason. He did this in the field as well as mounted; anything or anybody in his way was flattened. He dumped most of the people who rode him, and not once during the three months that I owned him was I able to mount him without help.

I really tried with the boy. He was only five. I took schooling very gently, trying to understand his problems. On the very last day of my three-month warranty, he finally deposited me from a great height on to my gravel yard during one of his indiscriminate charges.

On my visit to Accident and Emergency, with a headache worse than 10 hangovers, and a broken riding hat, I had plenty of time to decide he would not do in a riding school.

Honourably, the dealer took him back and agreed to find a replacement.

Over the following few weeks I looked at several more horses. There were odd-coloured ones, lumpy bumpy ones, wall eyes, wonky hocks, and tired nags that looked as if they had just been rounded up from a housing estate. It was all very dispiriting.

Then I got the call.

"Lucy. I have got you a horse. He has just arrived from the New Forest sales. He is perfect for you. Come quick. He won't be in the yard for long – I could sell him tomorrow."

That very afternoon, Alanna and a friend and I loaded ourselves into the Jeep and drove off to West Sussex again.

There he was – a handsome white grey with a little bit of pink on his muzzle and beautiful huge dark eyes.

"Oooh!" exclaimed the girls with one voice, "He looks just like a big Miranda. We MUST buy him!"

In fact Lynbrie Storm was lovely. We all had a ride in the school. He was 14 hands two inches, calm but not in an idle way, and had the best canter. I always maintain I bought him for that canter. He is a part-bred Welsh Cob, born in Wales in 2000 but early in his life he went to live on the Isle of Wight. I have no idea why he ended up at the New Forest sales and then at my dealer's yard. I did not ask. It was our lucky day!

I collected him the next afternoon.

As soon as he stepped off the ramp, I wormed him. I also kept him isolated from the others for three weeks. Hindsight is a wonderful thing!

Chapter Two.

Once his quarantine was up, Stormie thought he had landed in paradise. He fell in love with Bug and she with him. Bug had never been the flirty type but she was besotted! She neighed to him, could not take her eyes off him, and they grazed the paddock as one. Tippy thought he was pretty cool too. Miranda and Mia mostly ignored him. Killin wanted to give him a damn good kicking.

Killin therefore continued to live in another field with Lottie the livery. The other five spent the summer together in our field at Houndean Bottom. The field is old permanent pasture with good hedges and plenty of shelter. It worked really well. They sorted out a strict pecking order so feeding time and catching up time was not too hazardous. All was sweetness and light.

Riding Storm was a joy too. We have fabulous off-road riding on this part of the South Downs. I bought him to hack, so that is what we did.

His first outing was a short one to the sheep field gate accompanied by Killin and Tippy. Next I rode him along the Secret Valley with just Alanna and Tippy. Then it was all the way around the inside of the Lewes racecourse with Lottie. Then we did the Secret Valley again with Tippy and Lottie, where, much to his surprise, he encountered two small deer. He would get spooked easily so I made sure he always had a friend with him at this point. I was really enjoying myself – I am basically a happy hacker.

Gradually I began to use him to escort competent riders on the Downs. One such ride I remember well. We had been up through the woods in
Cuckoo Bottom, my client and Killin mostly
leading the way. On our way home the sea mist
rolled in. It can happen quite quickly – the lovely
sunny down land turns into something from a
scene from 'The Woman in Black'. The shrubs and
bushes take on a new menacing appearance as the
cold mist descends. Then horror of horrors! A
string of racehorses appeared ahead of us in the
fog. They were jogging and snorting, side stepping
and champing their bits. In one long line the
jockeys stood up in their stirrups and the racehorses began their canter up the steep hill away
from us. We could still just see them as they
reached the top, silhouetted against the skyline.
Stormie was beyond terrified, he was immobilised
by fear. I sat on him in that mist waiting for an
explosion. His heart was beating so fast and
loudly that I could hear it. He did not run. He
watched them canter out of sight, his poor heart
booming, his eyes like dinner plates.

We did make it home safely, hiding behind Killin,
who I must say behaved very well under the cir-
cumstances; in her youth she had a habit of taking
off in pursuit of racehorses. Storm was drenched in
sweat and very agitated. There are clearly few racehorses on the Isle of Wight.

These days he is pretty chilled about racehorses.
When they canter past us or cavort and buck along

the bridleway, he merely looks curiously and wonders why they are wasting all that energy.

It was very interesting to discover what things scared Storm and what did not. Cars, heavy machinery, tractors, the crop sprayer, cement mixer, chainsaws, lorries and buses were no problem. Pheasants, partridges, babies in buggies, sticks that might be snakes, people with backpacks, veterinary surgeons and having his face brushed were all absolutely terrifying.

Brushing his face was quite an issue. After some discussion and a couple of broken lead ropes, he let me do it, so long as I began on his neck going upwards, brushing around his ears and eventually down his face from the top. It was a necessity too. He had a special way of rolling which caused him to plaster mud over the front of his face between his eyes. We could not work out how he did it until one day I saw Miranda roll with the same result. While on her back during the roll over, she stretched her neck out long and rubbed her face in the mud, chin and throat uppermost. Most satisfying and very messy!

As well as being fun to hack, Storm was working well in the school and was amassing quite a fanbase. He was not Ottie but he was a pretty good substitute. His canter and slow collected trot were very popular. His perfect immobile square halt was his best thing. We called him The Queen's Drummer Horse.

Amazingly he could also jump.

Storm roared around my jumping field. He jumped anything and everything – bigger and wider each time. He certainly had ability and enthusiasm. He bounced at each obstacle like Tigger.

We were aghast! What on earth was this talented horse doing in my riding school?

Okay. So it was not exactly Hickstead, but he was impressive.

We took him to a jumping show at Plumpton College. He was a bit worried by the indoor school, with the noise and the hustle and bustle. Nevertheless, he managed many clear rounds. A bonus of going to Plumpton is that it is a really nice hack home over the Downs. Tippy had decided to go lame that very morning (how do horses know? How do they do that?). So, we quickly dusted Bug off and loaded her into the horse box instead. At 24 years old, Bug's proper jumping days were over so she did not compete. However, she was more than enthusiastic for the hack home. Alanna and little 14 hands high Bug led the way. Stormie was so happy.

Storm's first winter here was a proper one. Six inches of snow arrived on 18th December bringing with it temperatures of minus seven or eight degrees. Don't forget this is the sunny south east with its own temperate climate; horses and humans were equally surprised.

Walking down to the stables on the morning of first snow is a joy to behold. The world is stunningly beautiful and still belongs only to the rabbits, birds, foxes and deer which have left their foot-prints. There is an unusual muffled quietness only broken by excited neighs from hungry horses when I appear at the yard.

At first it was lots of fun – I like a bit of light-hearted disruption. Riding lessons were cancelled. Nobody went to school. Hot chocolate and brown-ies were for breakfast. Sledging down the hill in a haylage bag followed closely by a barking terrier took over as favoured sport.

The horses don't seem to mind the low tempera-ture; it is rain and wind together which really makes them cold and miserable. In the snow they played, rolled, reared and chucked out great hard snowballs from their hooves.

The snow kindly thawed for Christmas only to reappear in the New Year with a vengeance. Temperatures plummeted again. Where there had been a thaw, the roads and pathways were lethal sheets of ice. By Twelfth night, the south east was under a thick blanket of snow. Horses and most humans were going nowhere. The days consisted of feeding huge quantities of haylage, breaking ice on the water troughs, feeding more haylage, breaking more ice, defrosting the tap, feeding more haylage… You get the idea. Severe boredom was now setting in.

The thaw eventually came with heavy rain. This made the roads passable but my outdoor school, which in those days was just sand, was still a sheet of ice.

I was lucky enough to be able to hire the indoor school at the riding school next door. The indoor school at Hope in the Valley was one of the first two built in this country. The other was at Crabbet Park in Worth, West Sussex.

The school is a formidable building of wood with massive sliding doors and not much natural light. Even on a fine day it tends to be dark and a little gloomy. It was also haunted by a 'white lady' in the spectators' gallery, or so I was told as a child.

On this day, desperate to exercise the horses and earn some money, I gathered my posse of competent riders and five of my horses and took over the school. We knew they would be feeling lively. I did not expect the complete chaos that ensued.

Miranda was whizzing. Lottie was spooking and standing on end. Twenty-year-old Killin behaved like a four-year-old. Tippy practised her Quarter Horse standing starts and sliding stops. Storm discovered bucking.

His eyes gleamed. His coat glistened. He tossed his white mane and bucked all the way down the long side of the school. Every time the old wooden school creaked or groaned (or the white lady appeared), he would set off again. Yeee-ha! Everyone else joined in.

Incredibly no one fell off.

Chapter Three.

Things went from bad to worse over the next few months. Storm's bucking was very professional. His infamous 'one-two' (a huge buck to the right, immediately followed by another huge one to the left) became a regular feature of my lessons. He could even do 'one-two, three-four and FIVE' if you managed to stay on for the first ones.

He also stopped jumping. He was very sharp. He would stop in an instant at even the smallest fence and then celebrate with bucks. One poor girl (who loves him still) fell off him three times in one half-hour jumping lesson.

Often his buck would make him fart loudly, which terrified him and caused him to run away and buck. And then fart AGAIN. It was mayhem.

I know what you are thinking:

He must be in pain.
His feet must be sore.
His back is uncomfortable.
He does not like his bit.
His teeth hurt.
His eyesight is faulty.
His saddle does not fit.
He is getting too much food and not enough turn out…

I tried to address all these possibilities.

He did in fact have to have a wolf tooth out on the right-hand side. This entailed seven days off work which he thought was a good result.

The chiropractor treated his back and continues to treat him regularly.

My farrier pronounced his hooves healthy.

His eyes were checked by a vet.

I organised a brand-new Albion saddle to be fitted for him.

All my horses live on a grain free, high fibre diet. The Timothy haylage and Lucerne nuts are both meant to be good for their digestion and definitely not food that would make a horse fizzy. Storm lives out in a field, only coming in for a light breakfast and a lie down.

We also stopped jumping him completely. Of course we could have made him jump. I had plenty of riders who would have enjoyed the challenge but I felt a rest from it would be more beneficial. Maybe he had been over-jumped at his previous home?

Not every day was bad. Some days he would behave like a perfect gentleman, giving my riders a wonderful lesson or hack out.

Then the next he would be completely bonkers again.

It was about this time that I noticed his beautiful big dark eyes, which we were so taken by when we met him, were not as beautiful or big or dark as each other. His right eye definitely had more white in it which gave him a slightly mad appearance. Mad Eye Stormie we called him.

The new Albion saddle needed a second fitting. The flocking settles after a few weeks and may need attention. It was a very cold day in early May, an icy wind sweeping through my yard, when the saddler came to do the second fitting. The saddler likes to see the saddle on the horse without a numnah. He also likes to see someone ride in it.

I went to mount from my lovely high mounting block. As I made contact with the saddle, Storm took off: ONE-TWO! RIGHT-LEFT! There was an almighty crash as I hit the ground. The earth shook as far away as Hastings.

My face was planted in the gravel, in exactly the same place, for the second time in less than a year.

In that moment, I could have truly given up.

I won't pretend I was brave. I was shattered, sad and extremely sore. I tearfully asked the saddler if this had ever happened before.

"Oh yes," he said brightly. "Only last week I had a horse disappear off over Ditchling Common!"

(Note to self and anyone else who is interested: put a bloody saddle cloth on or, even better, a light pad.)

Now, I wholly admire horse riders who gallop off round National Hunt courses or fly round Badminton Horse Trials and the like. I really do. I admire their courage, fearless horsemanship and their fabulous horses.

I also like this definition of courage, attributed to John Wayne:

"*Courage is being scared to death but saddling up anyway.*"

I have often said it to myself over the years – exams, dentist appointments, job interviews, hip replacement...

Now I had to take it literally and apply it to saddling up Storm.

The thought of getting on him again gave me no pleasure. But, damn it, I knew he was not really mad or bad. My accident had just been incompetence by me and the saddler.

While Storm and I were falling out with each other, his popularity with my riders was increasing. He was, and is, of course, very charming.

Early on in his life at Houndean he showed us that he liked to be taken to the muck heap for a poo at about 9:30 in the morning. He would walk over to the heap, taking whoever was grooming him with him, back up and, with an audible push, do his poo.

He was incredibly neat in the stable. If his water bucket was not in the correct place, he would knock it over so it had to be replaced properly.

If the water was not perfectly clean or there was not quite enough of it, he would knock it over.

He always asks for a bucket of water while he is being groomed so he can have a drink. Then knocks it over.

Sometimes he just knocks water buckets over to amuse himself.

One astonishing day he finished his bucket feed, moved the bucket to the middle of the stable and peed in to it. No splash. No mess.

He was also very vocal. All his ablutions were accompanied by tuneful noises.

When he was hungry his neigh was squeaky and shrill – like he was going to faint if he does not get food NOW.

He will sort out your grooming kit for you.

Or tidy your coat and riding hat.

He knows every time you open the tub of mint imperials.

He can reshape a feed bucket to a design more to his liking.

He paws the ground with his right front hoof to tell you if you are not doing something quite right.

Never once have I seen him bite or kick or act aggressively towards a human being.

When we gradually introduced him to jumping again, we let him look at each fence before jumping. He would tentatively approach the poles, ears pricked, nose outstretched and knock it over. Everyone thought this was hilarious.

Except me.

And, yes, seven years on, we still let him inspect the jumps first because it entertains everyone and makes him happy.

Chapter Four.

Storm only dumped me twice more before I threw in the towel. The first time I was on a gentle stroll towards Cuckoo Wood with a client on Killin behind me. We were chatting. Some of my hacks are a bit of a 'coffee morning on horseback'. Lots of putting the world to rights and very relaxed. Perhaps a bit too relaxed. When a covey of partridges exploded out of the hedge, Storm did a speedy whip round and I landed in the ploughed field.

A few weeks later, with the same customer (oops!), I decided to take a slightly different path from the normal one coming home from the Battle of Lewes land. Storm did another 180-degree turn, this time more slowly, leaving me dangling at a 45-degree angle to the ground for what seemed like ages before he completed his turn and I had to drop off in to the bramble bush. Storm made his way back to our usual path and continued to walk slowly home. I do not think he noticed I had gone.

Apart from the thorns I was not hurt in either fall. I did conclude, however, that Storm was not going to be my escort horse. Not only were our antics unprofessional and embarrassing, – I am also too old to keep falling off!

As my wise horse chiropractor, who also treats me, said :

"Why put yourself through it, Lucy, when you have people who want to pay to ride him?"

So, Storm and I went our separate ways. He to the role of busy riding school horse, and I back to fighting my clients for the ride on Killin.

In fact, it began to work out quite well. Once Storm did not have to be lead horse he became a very reliable and fun hacker. One of the highlights of that summer was doing a three-hour ride which we called 'the S Bends'. I was on Killin, Alanna took Tippy, a friend rode Storm, and Pippa (my niece) rode Lottie the livery. The ride goes up the steep climb of Kingston Hill, down into the valleys behind with winding paths (hence the S Bends) and returns home going up Castle Hill and along Juggs Way. It is a stunningly beautiful route and that day seemed just about perfect. The sun shone and skylarks soared. Castle Hill is famous for its abundance of early spider orchids, but in August it is the most amazing place for butterflies – it was like a moving carpet of blues, whites and browns.

I think the only slight hazard of the trip was that I had to dismount and walk every now and again because my metal hips tend to seize up. Teetering on the edge of a water trough whilst trying to remount a rather excited Killin caused much hilarity. But I managed it without falling in – just adding to the enjoyment of a most fantastic day.

Because I am a riding school I have to keep an accident book. This means that every time someone falls off I have to fill in a form, get it signed, witnessed, record the casualty's comments, as well as treatment—if any—and follow-up treatment. It is then kept in a box file.

It was not like that when I learned to ride, let me tell you! In the 1960s, we all fell off all the time and got straight back on. You would not have dared do otherwise; the instructors were very frightening. You would not be considered 'a rider' until you had fallen off at least seven times. I remember falling off a little grey called Soda Pop three times on one hack. I had to run miles to catch him every time *and* my parents had to pay seventeen and sixpence for the exercise. No one thought it was odd.

Times change so I keep my accident book.

To make it more fun and to stop tearful children being so upset, we also keep a Horse Scores chart. Every time someone falls off, the horse scores a point. Miranda is 11 hands 2 inches, fast and feisty. She really wanted to be a Thoroughbred. She always gets the highest annual score and is proud of it. Except in Storm's first full year here when he doubled her score with an amazing twelve points!

The following summer we took a family holiday to America. Part of the holiday was to meet up with my Californian family that I had not seen in 30 years, and partly to spend a few days on a dude ranch in Montana near Yellowstone Park.

Riding in Montana was about as close to paradise as I have ever been. Riding those American Quarter horses up the mountain behind the ranch was incredible. The horses stepped up things, down things, over things and round things, negotiating obstacles which we would never even ask their British relatives to try. And all this with the sun beaming down, the snowy peaks of the Gallatin Mountains in the distance and the very slightest possibility that we might meet a bear. I was in love.

But I am getting side-tracked.

It is our trip to the rodeo which concerns Storm.

We were in West Yellowstone for the 4th July Independence Day Rodeo so I dragged my reluctant family along to it. Contrary to popular belief, it was well-run and very humane. The bronco would charge out of his pen, bucking like crazy with the cowboy on board. The cowboy usually stayed on for about three seconds after which the bronco was herded to the exit gate by two mounted wranglers and it trotted off to meet its friends again.

Back home in Sussex my few show jumps were set out in the field for the summer. Storm just could not help himself. He was jumping well and was very pleased with himself. On finishing his round, he would set off just like those broncos in Montana only better. Most of his riders fell off. However, I must put it on record here that every one of his riders stayed on a lot longer than the American cowboys: they were damn good! I was beginning to think we should be charging spectators to come and watch. We would have put on a grand show.

I suppose I should also add that I did not put anyone on him who did not want to ride him. He still had his ever-increasing fanbase.

But this is England and Storm's exuberant behaviour could not be allowed to continue. We swapped his nice French snaffle for a Dutch gag and put the reins on the second ring down. I cut down his food and tried to stage manage his lessons so he only ever being ridden with a sensible companion. It did help. A little.

Chapter Five.

Every year, on the anniversary of our mother's death, my sister Jo and I take a day off work and have a remembrance day.

We go on an outing or a trip to somewhere that we think she would have enjoyed. We talk about her a lot, reminisce and enjoy our memories. The plan has taken us on some odd adventures such as the London Orbital Overland train ride, which had come highly recommended. As the seats all face inwards and it gets dark early in January we did not see London, only each other. Very odd!

And then there was the trip to the Tate Modern to see a floor covered in sunflower seeds. What was that about? We felt sure our mother would have enjoyed it though.

This year we decided our mother would have liked to go to the Isle of Wight.

There had been much discussion and speculation amongst my riders and helpers about Storm's possible past. Why had he ended up at the New Forest sales? Had he been thrown off the Island for bad behaviour? Had there been one broken arm too many?

Jo and I set out to find his previous home, some clues, and seek some essence of Lynbrie Storm.

The Isle of Wight has a very posh pony club, one of the few in this country with its own premises. Some years ago, it appeared in the national press because parents were being accused of doping ponies belonging to rival children before pony club competitions. How true that is I have no idea – the press treated the story with sniggering amusement. The gist of the story was plain though: the Isle of Wight pony club was fiercely competitive.

Indeed, as we drove around the Island we were struck by the number of spacious houses with their own outdoor schools and beautifully fenced paddocks. There were swimming pools and tennis courts as well, but the number of houses with stables was impressive.

We made our way to the address which had been recorded on his passport. (Whether you love them or hate them, the current requirement for equine passports does make tracing your horses past a little easier). His previous home turned out to be a scrap yard – cars, trucks and all kinds of machinery stacked up. There did not appear to be a paddock, but that does not mean there wasn't one. It was not the sort of place that made me feel I could go in to ask if a handsome, snowy white horse had lived there a few years ago.

In truth, I think I was also a bit worried about what I might find out. I did not go in. Jo and I were still left with mostly speculation.

A scrap yard upbringing would certainly explain why Storm is not scared of machinery or vehicles. And possibly explains his worries about outdoorsy things—birds, snakes, squirrels, racehorses—and may be why he finds the need to kick and buck his way around my green and pleasant jumping field.

The highlight of the trip for me was the ferry ride. Jo and I sat at the front on both trips like a couple of schoolkids. There is a great view and I love all things boaty, particularly ocean-going ships. The Isle of Wight ferry was a reasonable substitute. I was fascinated to imagine Storm making the trip by ferry. He would have been three years old when he first set sail. What had he thought? Was he scared? Seasick? Missing his mum? Did the noise horrify him? Or perhaps he would have been interested in all things mechanical, inhaling the diesel fumes, savouring the smell of grease and the hum of the engine. Who knows?

It was certainly a far cry from the peace and quiet of the Welsh hills. I had previously found a picture of his sire in an old copy of the *Welsh Pony and Cob Stud Book*, and, with the information from his trusty passport, I had written to his breeder asking about his dam. I received no reply which also added to our general curiosity: had Storm been expelled from Wales on grounds of bad behaviour too, his breeder never wanting to hear of him again?

I think I am making it sound like he was a complete monster. He wasn't. For weeks on end he would behave impeccably. I even have some clients who have learned to ride on Storm who think he is a perfect Riding School Gentleman.

Happily he has always had a teenager who has been his special person. You have read *The Horse and His Boy* by C.S. Lewis? This was 'The Cob and

33

His Girl'. Storm did not actually speak – but very nearly. His communication was so good. His girl would take him for a long hack at least once a week in return for doing some poo picking. Poo picking is the clearing of all the horses droppings from the paddocks. It is done daily and is heavy work. The arrangement suited everyone. I got a bit of help with the chores, Storm and his girl had long exciting rides, and my pupils in the school were duped into thinking he was a school master. He is always more trustworthy the days after a fun ride out.

As well as this, he went to various events with his girls, who were competent riders, and his jumping was now reliable. He recently went to a jumping show, got in to the jump off but only came sixth because he did not really understand the speed thing. Rumour has it that he won the Most Ugly Cob class at an event. Surely that cannot be true?

He is also very versatile at the small shows that we do within the riding school. Sometimes it is jumping, sometimes it is games. One of my favourite games as a spectator is Fetch the Duck. Plastic ducks are placed at various heights on my jump wings around the school. Each competitor has to collect as many ducks as they can and pop them in the right bucket. The winner is obviously the rider with the most ducks. Storm sees things differently – he likes to knock the wings over and spray ducks about the place to lots of applause. It takes great riding skill to win Fetch the Duck on Storm.

Chapter Six.

Tippy is an American Quarter horse. She is the same age as Storm and much more sensible. Quarter horses tend to be intelligent, unflappable animals. They can turn their hoof to almost anything, as long as you explain things carefully they will understand and be helpful.

Some months after our wonderful holiday in Montana, my husband Tim was watching me turn Tippy out in the field, or bring her in, I can't remember. He must have been looking at her with new eyes because he said:

"Why don't you have a foal from her?"

It was a bit like the day when I was 15 and asked my parents if I could buy a foal for £20 and they said: "Yes."

I could not believe my ears. It was so unexpected!

No further encouragement was needed. I got straight on to my friend Ro, from whom I had bought Tippy as a five-year-old. She is an experienced breeder and has a wealth of knowledge about Quarter Horses.

After a fair bit of research, analysing videos of stallions, looking at blood lines, many telephone conversations with Ro and so on, we decided Tippy should visit a very handsome bay Quarter Horse stallion called Shiny Little Spark. Tim and I went to meet him at the stud in Devon first. Sparky was a gentleman. He was well-mannered, calm and friendly. Tippy packed her overnight kit and off she went to the West Country for a holiday.

Tippy's pregnancy and foaling is another story, but, suffice to say, those events had a major effect on Storm.

Tippy, who plans most things to her advantage, managed to prolong her romantic holiday to three months instead of the expected four weeks. Storm spent most of that summer living in Houndean Bottom with Bug, Miranda and Mia. Bug was still his special friend.

When Tippy returned, sleek and fat and beautiful, there was the dilemma: do I put my pregnant mare out with a gelding? There seemed to be so much conflicting advice.

The 'Never Put Your Pregnant Mare Out with a Gelding It Will Make Her Abort' camp was very vocal. Then there was the 'Nah! If She Knows the Gelding Well She Will Be Fine' lot. It was confusing.

In the end, I decided she should go out in the field as usual with Storm and co. After all she had lived with him for three years before going off to stud and not being with her friends would be distressing. I also tend to think that if it is a healthy, strong foetus, it is unlikely to be aborted, and if it is aborted, there was probably something not quite right with it.

Everything seemed to be fine. There was much

snorting and pawing the ground when Tippy returned to the paddock but it was short lived and soon became no more than a greeting with swan necks whenever they met.

I did not really notice any changes in behaviour, but, looking back now, I think Storm did become a bit more protective of Tippy.

* * *

Anyone who has looked after multiple horses in a field knows how difficult it can be to bring one in without all the others wanting to come too; gate-ways become hazardous and mine are no different. Early morning, I bring all my horses in for their breakfast and lie down before their work begins for the day. Bug, Storm, Tippy, Miranda, Mia had their strict pecking order which made my job just about manageable.

Bug came in first as she was the boss. Then I would collect Storm and Tippy together, followed by Miranda and Mia. We had an unsettled autumn with heavy rainfall and strong winds. Storm's behaviour became more and more erratic when I was bringing him in. I am very right-handed so I always held his rope in that hand with Tippy plod-ding amiably on my left side. Leaving the field, we have to negotiate a sometimes-muddy grassy track alongside a bridleway and farm road. Then there is a Dutch barn with straw, sheds, a builders' skip, a hazel tree, a white rose, possibly puddles, birds, nettles, thistles, a terrier, possibly a wheelbarrow – nothing—you would think—that could be remotely scary.

Storm began spooking at *things*. The *things* were usually just behind him wherever we happened to be. I have said before – he is very sharp. His spooks were doubly sharp. He would just leap up and pull backwards (why backwards? Towards the scary *thing*? No, I don't know either). But it had maximum effect on my control. Mostly I managed to keep hold of him but not without him painfully wrenching my arm up and backwards too.

As with most behavioural problems, if not nipped in the bud, it becomes a big issue. I began dreading bringing him in so I now arrived at the gate each morning with barely concealed apprehension. And don't horses always know when we are nervous? It makes them nervous too because there must be *something* to be nervous of! Normally with a spooker, I give the horse the benefit of the doubt: even if I cannot see the scary *thing*, I believe the horse can. I don't make a big deal out of it. I try and ignore it and I would never punish a horse for getting spooked. Fear and flight is in their DNA and has kept them off the endangered list for millions of years.

* * *

On a Saturday in early November, Bug seemed a bit off colour. It had been hideous weather (as usual) and I thought she must be chilled. I kept her stabled for the weekend, tempting her to eat with small feeds and mint. She perked up a bit on Sunday. On Monday she was rushed off to the veterinary hospital. On Tuesday Bug was dead.

I have been in the company of horses long enough to know that they do mourn their friends. Some people suggest to me that they are actually reflecting our mood. I think there is more to them than that. As we battled with the wind, the rain, the dark and the sadness, a steady gloom descended upon my yard.

Storm's morning behaviour got worse. There were scary *things* everywhere. I tried bringing him in by himself, but that only caused mayhem in the field as Tippy roared up and down the fence line until I came back to get her. Her galloping and sliding stops in the mud were more than my nerves could stand. I bought Storm in wearing his bridle. Sometimes I used a lunge rein. Occasionally I would lose him completely and with a loud clatter of metal on tarmac he would charge off to his stable.

Yes, it was very tempting to let him bring himself in every morning. But that would have been stupid, wouldn't it? Imagine if he ran someone over or crashed into a car... It would not have been good for his discipline either, so we grumpily battled on, eyeing each other ever more warily each morning.

Chapter Seven.

Soon after Bug's untimely death, my 90-year-old father invited me for our usual early Sunday evening glass of wine at his house. He is not a horse person. My parents became sort-of horse people only because of my passion and because all their seven grandchildren took up riding at some point.

That evening he said:

"I want to buy myself a New Forest pony and lend it to you indefinitely."

How can you beat that for an offer? It was such a wonderful thought and he had a typically special way of putting it. He knew—without being told—that losing Bug was difficult for my riding school.

Setting out to buy a pony is not my favourite thing (see the beginning of this book!) but I began putting out some feelers. I wanted a middle-aged pony that I could use in the riding school straight away.

I was offered several New Forest ponies over the next few months but they were all young or green or needed bringing on. Not really what I had in mind. Besides, I had a foal due in the summer which would be in need of training.

I was on the phone to Ro bemoaning this fact while she was telling me she really could not face another winter looking after horses. It was at this point when we both had a 'light bulb' moment.

Would Shonie the Pony like to come and live with me? Could she take to riding school work? It suddenly became hugely exciting and my father thoroughly approved of buying a pony from Ro!

Donatus Shona arrived on Easter Sunday. Not a New Forest pony, but a beautiful 14 hands 2 inches Welsh Cob, sixteen years old, dark bay with a blaze, socks, and a delightful temperament. Shona is a ride-and-drive pony – driving being Ro's favoured sport. Shona is still with me; she took to riding school life like a duck to water.

Storm was horrified. He absolutely could not bear the sight of her. Obviously, I kept them well separated, but if Shona was led past his stable or near his field gate, he would charge at her – ears back, teeth bared looking like the horse from hell.

Working them together was safe enough as Storm always had a competent rider on board. I also think that while they were working, Storm did not feel she was such a threat to him.

As the time for Tippy's foaling came closer, I decided to move Tippy in to the largest stable at night and keep her away from Storm. She agreed with this plan and spent long, sleepy nights indoors and peaceful, grassy days in the paddock with Killin.

Shona was spending a lot of time out with Mia and Miranda, but not yet with Storm. However, the long-term plan was to have all four Welsh living together. One calm Friday evening when lessons were over, I decided to turn Storm out with the mares. I was expecting a bit of hierarchy interaction (there always is) but was not overly concerned. No one had back shoes on (especially taken off for the occasion) so I did not foresee any damage.

Nothing happened for forty minutes. Shona and Storm stayed at different ends of the paddock. Mia and Miranda grazed as always.

Then suddenly Storm charged.

He galloped at Shona with a face like one of the four horses of the apocalypse. She took off fast, kicking out at him with both hind hooves. She really did try her best to retaliate. I held my nerve for what seemed like ages. Hoping they would call a truce and calm down as usually happens.

This was different. Storm was enraged, swift on his feet and had a lethal way of chasing Shona into a corner to attack. She escaped him many times. Immediately he was off and at her again. Actually, he was not just attacking. He was going for the kill. A couple of times he nearly had her on the ground. It was the most appalling thing to watch. I have never before—or since—seen a horse behave as he did. Not even in a film.

My weekend helpers had been watching with me, and one of the mums turned up. With a bucket of pony nuts we managed to distract Storm long enough to get Shona out of the gate. The poor girl was dripping with sweat, shaking and near to exhaustion. I promised her there and then that I would never, ever let Storm in the same field as her again.

Between us we got Shona and Storm round to the stable yard. He was also in a terribly distressed state. We washed them down and tended to the bite marks and kicks. Amazingly the wounds were all superficial. Not so the emotional trauma. That was severe and deep.

"Is he a rig?" asked several people. A rig is an incompletely castrated horse. Although a rig may look like a gelding, there are one or both testicles hidden up inside the abdomen. A rig behaves like a stallion.

Up until the arrival of Shona, Storm had shown no aggressive or stallion-like behaviour. Surely, if he were a rig, he would be trying to mate with Shona, not kill her?

Whatever was going on in his head – I had a problem.

Some weeks after the Shona incident, Mia and he happened to have the same morning off work so I popped them out in the paddock together. Before I could even say,

"But they lived happily together for four years…" he was off and at her, charging her with teeth and front hooves. Luckily Mia was small and speedy and I was ready. She galloped straight back out of the opened the gate.

I had one more try at finding Storm an acceptable companion. Lottie the livery had always loved him from afar. He always called out to her when she arrived at the outdoor school and vice versa. Lottie was quite flirtatious in his company. If they went for a hack together they got as close to each other as stirrups and feet would allow. She always admired his crazy antics in school lessons and tried to join in whenever she could. Storm had never shown any animosity towards Lottie at all. So, with permission, we decided to give it a go.

At first their relationship in the field was very entertaining. Lottie was so passionate about Storm that *she* chased *him*. It was a pleasure to watch.

Peace did not last long. Although she still seemed enamoured of Storm, a more-than-normal number of bite marks were appearing on Lottie. They went briefly to live in the field next to my outdoor school. When I went to put them in their stables at night more often than not I would find Lottie in the school and Storm pacing outside. Clearly she had jumped the fence to escape him. Damn and blast the horse! Storm I mean, not Lottie.

The only action was for Storm to live as a bachelor – completely and utterly. He could not even be in a field next to mares because he still charged at them over the flint wall, damaging himself, the wall and possibly the mares. He could have jumped the wall with ease had it occurred to him. It made no difference if the mares were in season – Storm wanted to attack them any time, any place.

From that day, Storm lived alone in the football pitch. It is a little paddock which got its name because our children who, when they were small, used to use the field shelter with their friends as a goal for practising penalty shootouts. It is well-fenced with post and rail with an electric wire running in it and the flint wall. There is an empty field, then the mares' field. It is quite ridiculous really – even to this day I have to make sure he has his head in a bucket of feed when I lead the girls past his patch. Timing must be perfect.

The extra work was exhausting. I seemed to spend so much time just moving ponies and horses around from stable to field, and football pitch to field (Storm had to go and have some grass some-times) and back to stables again. Then it was mares back to the field. I walked miles—including the miles I walk when I am teaching—all the time making sure Storm was not anywhere near any one. It was a hard winter. I was permanently anxious and dreaded the carnage that I might find in the mornings.

Miranda was not wintering well.

I try and keep my horses living outside as much as possible – even at night in the winter with good shelter and rugs if necessary. It is the most natural way and they are generally healthier, happier and better behaved. However, this winter Miranda needed a stable. She was quite skinny under her thick Welsh Mountain coat. I wondered if Shona was stopping Miranda getting as much feed and shelter as she was used to. Miranda seemed happy to live in anyway, something that she would have hated in years gone by.

With my limited space, this meant Storm lived out at night in his football pitch. He was a bit surprised to begin with, but seemed to settle in reasonably well. I think he liked to stroll around and keep an eye on his patch.

Chapter Eight.

One morning in January, I arrived at the yard in semi-darkness. Something was not quite right. There was a big shape up against the stable block. It took me a few moments to realise it was Storm in his black outdoor rug with his head over the door talking to Tippy. What a sight! He had trashed his fence, negotiated a telegraph pole and wire, stepped over a pile of building flints, rolled on the muck heap, done two poos on the muck heap, and gone to talk to Tippy.

See how he can charm you? Just when you think he is the worst, most difficult horse in the world and it is about time he found another home, he persuades you that he is clever, tidy and really, really wants to live here.

The yard gate was open at night in those days. Storm could have gone anywhere. He could have gone to visit the high life of Brighton. He could have found Shona and Mia and beaten them up. He could have made his way to the feed bins, eaten his fill and given himself colic. He could have found himself a nice, safe scrap yard to live in.

But no, he chose to stay right here and talk to Tippy.

Tim reinforced his fencing, bought new batteries for the electric wire, and we kept the yard gate shut.

Tippy's foal, Scout, had been born in the previous July. By January, I was strongly advised by the vets and my farrier to wean her. I had not intended to do it until the spring, but Scout was growing too quickly and might be doing herself damage. Tippy was a bit thin. If I upped her food, it only made Scout fatter; Tippy was a surprisingly good cow.

Fifty years ago my stables were cattle pens. They are big and the horses can talk to each other over the partition walls. The walls are far too high to jump but it did mean that when I put Scout in a separate stable she could still see and sniff noses with her mother. I weaned very slowly: first twenty minutes, then fifty minutes, gradually rising to all night and separate paddocks by day. Killin was a fabulous aunty to Scout which definitely made weaning easier.

However, weaning did mean that little Scout was taking up another precious, big stable. Miranda was still living in and had even had an unexplained bout of colic which was a big worry. Lottie the livery was living in the other big stable at night but it was difficult to know what to do with her during the day. She could not go out with Storm and she could not have Killin because Scout needed Killin. My days just seemed to be an endless, not very happy game of musical stables and paddocks. I think I even found time to do some teaching some days.

My right arm became excruciatingly painful. I politely called it 'poo pickers arm' but really I blame it almost entirely on Storm. I developed a technique of holding my coat collar with my right arm when I dismounted from a horse. This is also a useful technique for ladies of a certain age suffering from a frozen shoulder. If you have had one, you will know what I mean!

Like a true Brit I make brief notes about the weather in my work diary. I only note it if it is extreme, unusual or particularly special in any way. It is interesting to look back on my entries for the beginning of 2014. I don't say much except the occasional "sunshine!" or "it didn't rain all day!" or "sunny for three hours!" In other words, the first three months of that year were abysmal – so bloody wet and windy that it had become normal.

Spring did arrive eventually of course. With the warmer weather, the ponies and riders cheered up, behaviour improved and I was very slightly less tired. I gave notice to Lottie's owners that I would not be able to keep her here next winter. It was a big and sad decision to make; something had to change before September and Lottie was the only pony who did not belong to me. It took Lottie five months to find a new home. In some ways that was no bad thing as it meant she spent the best of the summer here enjoying the hacking, jumping, pony care sessions and silly games that happen in riding schools during the long days. Oh yes – and don't forget the serious equitation lessons.

Storm was working well in every way. His lateral work was improving and, instead of the 'square halt' being his best thing, his 'turn on the forehand' became his show off party piece. Okay, so it did not require him to move much.

He was a lovely boy out on the Downs. He rarely got spooked. He bounced off into canter with lots of enthusiasm. This only lasted five or six strides but his riders loved him. If you worked really hard he would bounce off into canter again!

There was a Sunday in June which began as it always does. Storm is the first one to have breakfast. He is very vocal while I am getting it ready; shrill and squeaky, his stomach is touching his backbone. I opened the gate of the football pitch and he came trotting in for his food. All his normal behaviour. After breakfast he had his nap.

Pippa got him ready for lessons. He took her to the muck heap for his poo at 9:30. Then the other ponies and pupils and he went off to the outdoor school as usual. I did my first half-hour lesson. During my second lesson Pippa came to tell me that Storm seemed to have some bites on him. By the time I took a good look at him he was very lumpy. Having abandoned the lessons, we walked him home. At the stable yard he was covered in hives all over his body and very distressed.

He paced his stable. He pawed the ground. He rolled. He sweated. He lay down. He got back up. He paced and pawed and rubbed his body on the stable walls. His face and muzzle swelled.

Soon his face was swollen grotesquely – huge

with little piggy eyes and taut skin. I dread to think what was going on in his mouth and throat.

At this point Storm gave up. He lay down to die.

The wait for an emergency vet is always interminable. In fact she arrived within half an hour. He was injected with a monster dose of anti-inflammatory drugs.

And then we waited.

The vet could shed no real light on what could have caused such a sudden and dramatic allergic reaction. Apparently we often never discover the cause. It was more likely to be a sting than something he ate.

For me, this episode was a turning point. Storm looked so vulnerable and sore and worried for himself that I actually felt sorry for him. Maybe he was not the demon I thought he was. I realised I really did not want him to die. I did not even want to sell him. I wanted him to recover. I wanted him to be completely better. I wanted to make him a happy, content, loving, well-behaved horse.

The anti-inflammatories kicked in and Storm did get better. It took days for his swollen face to return to normal, but his appetite was back by the next morning.

So 'Project Keeping Stormie Happy' began.

He continued to live alone in the football pitch. He came in to his stable daily for his nap. He also always spent some time out in the big grassy field of Houndean Bottom. Here he could have a good old buck and kick when he felt like it. All the time he was separate from the mares.

I think he liked his solitude. He did not have to argue with anyone over food or space or shelter. There were no scary hormonal mares to confuse him. It was like all his anxieties had been taken away. It was suggested I get him Sky Sports and some lagers to complete his contentment.

Lager not being available, he got vegetables. Aware that he was eating less grass than the mares, we let Storm have all the spare raw veggies from the kitchen. He looked forward to his colander of goodies appearing by the fence at about 7pm.

He likes: carrots, parsnips, turnips, broccoli, cauliflower, swede, cabbage (loves cabbage!) and of course apples and pears.

No celeriac, potatoes or salad leaves, which are not good for horses' tummies. And definitely no sprouts – not good for man nor beast, he says.

We also bought him a horse ball. He was not much interested, preferring playthings of his own choice.

In the past, bringing Storm in from the big field had been a real problem. Because he was now on his own I made a deal with myself: if he misbehaves, let go! Not my usual course of action but my right arm was completely shot and I dared not wreck it any more. I went to collect Storm with just a rope around his neck. I made sure his stable door (and only his) was propped open. He was as good as gold. There may well have been spooky things on the way in, but he took no notice. He plodded by my side.

Coming in from the football pitch was just too easy. Open door, open gate, stroll in for breakfast. It worked in reverse going out for supper in the evening. The Horse Scores were proof that Stormie was becoming incredibly chilled. Only three pupils fell off him that year and one of those was a slither.

My painful arm settled down to something commonly known as Popeye arm. My champion arm wrestling days are over and it looks a bit of an odd shape, but it does not hurt. Bliss!

Chapter Nine.

Storm celebrated his 15th birthday in 2015. I do not know his exact date of foaling so he shares Tippy's birthday, 18th May. Tippy was also a millennium foal.

I have often said that riding school horses become most useful at age 15. They know their job. They are used to being ridden by many different people and are fairly unflappable. Mine are totally in tune with my body language by this time and understand all my voice commands. Teaching more experienced riders, I sometimes resort to code – just to make sure the horse is listening to the rider. In beginner lessons, it is great having a yard full of attentive, well-behaved school masters. And so Storm proved to be. He was the perfect angel. I was feeling pretty smug.

Storm hit the big time that year. Not only was it the year I began writing his memoirs (yes, it really did take that long), but he also had his portrait drawn and exhibited.

My cousin Simon is an artist. He wished to draw the musculature of a horse and I had just the chap for the job.

Simon intended to draw the horse from photographs. The pictures had to be taken in semi-darkness with lights provided by Simon. So, one evening after an early supper and a glass of wine, a posse of people descended on Storm and his football pitch. Storm had to stretch his neck long and upwards or long and round to reach an apple. Several pictures were taken and Storm was expert at reaching for apples. Lights, camera, fame, and admiration did not bother him at all. The resulting drawings were also very good indeed.

In 2015, I extended my riding school insurance to include unaccompanied hacking. For the month of August, Storm was part-loaned to two sisters who love him. He stayed here living in his patch but went on lots of exciting and different hacks. He went to Black Cap, Ashcombe Bottom and visits to Kingston and Kingston Hill. He only did a few school lessons that month. When he did, he was a bit lazy. No matter.

"Better lazy than crazy," we all nodded happily and patted ourselves on the back.

Summer turned to autumn. Storm was still chilled. He began taking some more novice rides in lessons. Even some pupils who had been slightly in awe of him were requesting to ride him.

Bonfire night, which is big in Lewes, came and went. On the fifth, instead of doing his poos in the top right hand corner of his patch, he did them in the bottom left corner so he could watch the many aerial firework displays.

The weather was rainy and windy for most of November and December. My only notable comment in my weather diary was on Christmas Eve when I wrote: "Dry afternoon and beautiful moon".

It must have been unusual.

On New Year's Eve I had three lessons. Two quiet ones with Shona and one mother and daughter combination on Tippy and Storm. Mother and daughter are both competent riders and all was going as it should. There was a minor issue getting Tippy in to canter at the correct moment when all of a sudden, quite out of the blue, Storm bucked. He pinged his rider right over his head.

A week later he did it again with someone else.

A fortnight after that Storm surpassed himself.

It was the last lesson of a busy Saturday morning. Shona was doing the world's slowest walk (it is her speciality), Mia was wandering aimlessly around the outdoor school with a child who had forgotten how to steer, and Tippy was probably nibbling the hawthorn and humming a tune. It was a riding teacher's nightmare. How to get this lot sorted out?

Storm watched carefully, taking it all in. His inappropriate sense of humour kicked in; from his famous square halt, Storm bucked straight upwards about three meters in a perfect U shape. He never ceases to surprise; I have never seen a horse buck quite like that either. His teenage rider soared another three meters into the air before landing unhurt on the rubber chips.

In February he decided to liven up a jumping lesson. His rider was experienced and enjoying herself. We were on our last little bit of the lesson: a double with a small spread on the second jump. He bounced at it with lots of enthusiasm. Cleared both bits with ease, bucked on landing, plonked his rider in the dusty corner, tucked his head between his knees and belted off around the school.

BUCK BUCK BUCKETY BUCK! Off went Storm doing his *very* best thing.

Did I dare to say I thought I had him worked out?

About the author

Lucy Postgate's horse riding career began as a young child playing ponies cantering around her London bedroom. After the family moved to East Sussex Lucy began to learn to ride real ponies at Hope in the Valley Riding School in Lewes. She was aged ten. Lucy went on to take and pass her BHSAI in 1975 and has been running her own riding school since 1977. Lucy is married to Tim Duffield. They have two grown up children, George and Alanna.

Lightning Source UK Ltd.
Milton Keynes UK
UKOW04n1928030917
308499UK00001B/1/P